Sheffield Wedn

Quiz Book

101 Questions That Will Test Your Knowledge Of This Great Football Club

Published by Glowworm Press
7 Nuffield Way
Abingdon OX14 1RL

By Chris Carpenter

Sheffield Wednesday FC

This book contains one hundred and one informative and entertaining trivia questions with multiple choice answers. With 101 questions, some easy, some more challenging, this entertaining book will test your knowledge and memory of the club's long history.

You will be asked questions on a wide range of topics associated with Sheffield Wednesday Football Club for you to test yourself. You will be quizzed on players, legends, managers, opponents, transfer deals, trophies, records, honours, fixtures, songs and much more. Both enjoyable and educational, the Sheffield Wednesday FC Quiz Book will provide the ultimate in entertainment for Wednesdayites of all ages, and will test your knowledge of **Sheffield Wednesday** and prove you really know your club well.

2022/23 Season Edition

FOREWORD

When I was asked to write a foreword to this book I was honoured.

I have known the author Chris Carpenter for a number of years and his knowledge of facts and figures is phenomenal.

His love for football and his talent for writing quiz books makes him the ideal man to pay homage to my great love Sheffield Wednesday Football Club.

This book came about as a result of a challenge on a golf course.

I do hope you enjoy the book.

David Hutchison

Let's start with some relatively easy questions.

1. When were Sheffield Wednesday founded?
     A. 1866
     B. 1867
     C. 1868

2. What is Sheffield Wednesday's nickname?
     A. The Kestrels
     B. The Kites
     C. The Owls

3. Who has made the most appearances for the club in total?
     A. Jack Brown
     B. Alan Finney
     C. Andrew Wilson

4. Who is the club's record goal scorer?
     A. John Fantham
     B. David Hirst
     C. Andrew Wilson

5. Who or what is the club mascot?
     A. Oddy Owl
     B. Oswald Owl
     C. Ozzie Owl

6. What is the Sheffield Wednesday Supporters Society also known as?
     A. The Dreamers

B. High Society

C. The Wednesdayites

7. What is the address of Sheffield Wednesday's website?
    A. owls.co.uk
    B. swfc.co.uk
    C. wednesday.co.uk

8. What is the club's motto?
    A. In Pursuit of Excellence
    B. Work Conquers All
    C. By Wisdom and Courage

9. What song do the players run out to?
    A. Bright Eyes
    B. Super Trouper
    C. Waterfront

10. Which of these is a well known pub near the ground?
    A. The Night Owl
    B. The Owls Nest
    C. The Rawson Spring

OK, here are the answers to the first ten questions. You will need a good start as the questions will get harder.

A1. Sheffield Wednesday was founded on 4th September 1867.

A2. Sheffield Wednesday's nickname is The Owls.

A3. Scottish forward Andrew Wilson made the most appearances for the club, with 560 in total. He played for the club from 1900 to 1920, and he was 39 years old when he played his last game for the club.

A4. Andrew Wilson is also the club's record goal scorer with 216 goals to his name.

A5. Over the years, the club have had several Owl themed match day mascots. Originally it was Ozzie the Owl, and later Baz and Ollie were introduced. All three were replaced by Barney Owl in 2006. In January 2009, Ozzie Owl was re-introduced as the main mascot, with Barney relegated to a secondary role. In 2012, Ollie Owl returned with a remit to work with the "children in the community" programme. Today, Ozzie Owl is recognised as the official club mascot.

A6. The Sheffield Wednesday Supporters Society is better known as the Wednesdayites.

A7. swfc.co.uk is the club's official website address.

A8. The club's motto is 'By Wisdom and Courage'.

A9. The Wednesday players run out to the song Waterfront by Simple Minds.

A10. The Rawson Spring is a well-known pub near the ground. Be prepared to queue for a pint though.

Now let's have some ground related questions.

11. Where does Sheffield Wednesday play their home games?
     A. Myrtle Road
     B. Hillsborough Stadium
     C. Owlerton Stadium

12. What is the stadium's current capacity?
     A. 34,854
     B. 35,854
     C. 36,584

13. What is the name of the road the ground is on?
     A. Don Lane
     B. Lemmings Lane
     C. Penistone Road

14. Which stand has the biggest capacity?
     A. North Stand
     B. South Stand
     C. Spion Kop

15. What is the traditional "home" end of the ground known as?
     A. Cantilever End
     B. Leppings Lane End
     C. Spion Kop

16. What is the club's record attendance?
     A. 70,841

B. 72,841
C. 74,841

17. Who were the opponents for the club's record attendance?
    A. Liverpool
    B. Manchester City
    C. Manchester United

18. What is the size of the pitch?
    A. 115 x 70 yards
    B. 116 x 71 yards
    C. 117 x 75 yards

19. How many FA Cup semi-finals has Hillsborough hosted?
    A. 23
    B. 25
    C. 27

20. Where is Sheffield Wednesday's training ground?
    A. Chesterfield Road
    B. Middlewood Road
    C. Northumberland Street

Here are the answers to the last block of questions.

A11. The club plays their home games at Hillsborough Stadium.

A12. The stadium's maximum capacity is 34,854; and although it has been constantly reduced over the years, it is one of the largest football stadiums in England outside of the Premier League.

A13. Hillsborough Stadium is on Penistone Road.

A14. The South Stand has the largest capacity, seating up to 11,352 people.

A15. The Spion Kop end is where the most vocal Wednesday supporters sit.

A16. The club's record attendance is 72,841.

A17. The match with the record attendance was an FA Cup Fifth round tie at home to Manchester City on 17th February 1934. The match ended in a 2-2 draw.

A18. The pitch is 116 yards long and 71 yards wide. By way of comparison, the pitch at Wembley Stadium is 115 yards long and 75 yards wide.

A19. Hillsborough has hosted 27 FA Cup semi-finals in total.

A20. Sheffield Wednesday's training ground is on Middlewood Road.

Let's move onto the next set of questions.

21. What is the club's record win in any competition?
    A. 11-0
    B. 12-0
    C. 13-0

22. Why is the club called Wednesday?
    A. The founding members had their day off work on Wednesday
    B. After Lord Wednesday
    C. It was named after a local colliery

23. On Boxing Day 1979 Wednesday beat Sheffield United by what score?
    A. 2-0
    B. 3-0
    C. 4-0

24. What is the club's record win in the league?
    A. 7-1
    B. 8-1
    C. 9-1

25. Who did they beat in that record win?
    A. Birmingham City
    B. Blackburn Rovers
    C. Bristol Rovers

26. In which season was the record win?

A. 1931/32
B. 1932/33
C. 1933/34

27. What is the club's record defeat?
    A. 0-8
    B. 0-9
    C. 0-10

28. What is the furthest the club has progressed in a
    major European competition?
    A. Last 32
    B. Last 16
    C. Last 8

29. Who is currently Head of Recruitment?
    A. Charlie Baker
    B. David Downes
    C. Richard Higgins

30. Which of these Trevors played for Sheffield
    Wednesday?
    A. Trevor Eve
    B. Trevor Francis
    C. Trevor McDonald

Here are your answers to the last ten questions.

A21. The club's record win in any competition is a whopping 12-0, when Halliwell FC (from Greater Manchester) were thrashed in the first round of the FA Cup on 18th January 1891.

A22. The club is so named because it was on Wednesdays that the founding members had their day off work.

A23. The Boxing Day Massacre was a Football League Third Division match which took place on 26th December 1979, when a record Third Division crowd of 49,309 supporters watched Wednesday beat United 4-0.

A24. The club's record win in the League is 9-1.

A25. This comfortable victory came against a struggling Birmingham City side.

A26. Wednesday beat Birmingham City 9-1 during the 1933/34 season.

A27. The club's record defeat is 0-10, which was in a Division One match away to Aston Villa on 5th October 1912.

A28. Sheffield Wednesday reached the quarter finals of the Inter-Cities Fairs Cup (a predecessor to the Europa

League) in 1962, before losing to Barcelona 3-4 on aggregate.

A29. David Downes is currently employed as Head of Recruitment.

A30. Trevor Francis made 76 appearances for Wednesday between 1990 and 1994.

Now we move onto some questions about some of the club's trophies.

31. How many times have Sheffield Wednesday won the First Division league title?
    A. 3
    B. 4
    C. 5

32. How many times have Sheffield Wednesday won a league title (all leagues)?
    A. 7
    B. 8
    C. 9

33. How many times have Sheffield Wednesday won the FA Cup?
    A. 2
    B. 3
    C. 4

34. How many times have Wednesday won the League Cup?
    A. 1
    B. 2
    C. 3

35. How many times have Wednesday won the Community Shield?
    A. 1
    B. 2

C. 3

36. When did the club win their first Division One league title?
    A. 1902/03
    B. 1903/04
    C. 1904/05

37. When did the club last win the first Division One league title?
    A. 1928/29
    B. 1929/30
    C. 1930/31

38. When did the club win their first ever FA Cup?
    A. 1894
    B. 1895
    C. 1896

39. When did the club last win the FA Cup?
    A. 1931
    B. 1933
    C. 1935

40. Who was the last captain to lift the FA Cup?
    A. Mark Hooper
    B. Wilf Sharp
    C. Ronnie Starling

Here are the answers to the last set of questions.

A31. Sheffield Wednesday have won the First Division 4 times

A32. Sheffield Wednesday have won 9 League titles in total. They have won the Second Division 5 times and the First Division 4 times.

A33. The club has won the FA Cup 3 times: 1896, 1907 and 1935.

A34. Sheffield Wednesday have won the League Cup just the once. What a glorious day that was.

A35. Sheffield Wednesday have won the Community Shield, or Charity Shield as it was then known, once; back in 1935.

A36. The Wednesday, as the club was then known, won their first Division One league title in 1902/03.

A37. Sheffield Wednesday last won the first Division One league title in 1929/30.

A38. The Wednesday, as the club was then known, beat Wolverhampton Wanderers 2-1 in the 1896 FA Cup final on the 18th April 1896 which was held at the old Crystal Palace. Fred Spiksley scored both the goals.

A39. The last time the club won the FA Cup was when Wednesday beat West Bromwich Albion 4-2 in the final on 27th April 1935 at Wembley Stadium.

A40. Ronnie Starling was the captain who lifted the FA Cup that Spring afternoon.

I hope you're having fun, and getting most of the answers right.

41. What is the record transfer fee paid?
    A. £6 million
    B. £8 million
    C. £10 million

42. Who was the record transfer fee paid for?
    A. Paolo Di Canio
    B. Adam Reach
    C. Jordan Rhodes

43. What is the record transfer fee received?
    A. £2.5 million
    B. £3 million
    C. £3.5 million

44. Who was the record transfer fee received for?
    A. Chris Brunt
    B. Mark Hooper
    C. Kevin Pressman

45. Who was the first Sheffield Wednesday player to play for England?
    A. Billy Betts
    B. Billy Brayshaw
    C. Billy Mosforth

46. Who has won the most international caps whilst a Sheffield Wednesday player?

A. Alan Finney
B. Andrew Wilson
C. Nigel Worthington

47. What is the highest number of goals that Wednesday has scored in a league season?
    A. 104
    B. 105
    C. 106

48. Who is the youngest player ever to represent the club?
    A. Peter Fox
    B. Martin Hodge
    C. Don Megson

49. Who is the oldest player ever to represent the club?
    A. Mark Hooper
    B. Jerry Jackson
    C. Henry Miller

50. How much did Sheffield Wednesday pay for Chris Waddle?
    A. £500,000
    B. £750,000
    C. £1 million

Here are the answers to the last block of questions.

A41. Sheffield Wednesday's highest transfer fee paid is £10 million.

A42. This fee was paid to Middlesbrough on 1st July 2017 for striker Jordan Rhodes.

A43. The record transfer amount received for a player at the club is £3 million.

A44. £3 million was received for Chris Brunt from West Bromwich Albion on 15th August 2007. There were add-ons to the sale of Darko Kovacevic that may have passed this figure, but the official line is that Chris Brunt is the club's record sale.

A45. Billy Mosforth was the first Wednesday player to play for England. He made his debut in March 1877 and went on to play nine times for his country, scoring three goals.

A46. Nigel Worthington has won the most international caps whilst a Sheffield Wednesday player. He won 50 of his 66 caps for Northern Ireland whilst playing for the club between 1984 and 1994.

A47. Sheffield Wednesday scored an incredible 106 goals in total during the 1958/59 season.

A48. Goalkeeper Peter Fox is the youngest player to ever represent the club, aged just 15 years and 8 months when he made his debut back in 1972.

A49 Jerry Jackson is the oldest player to ever represent the club, aged an incredible 46 years old when he turned out against Port Vale on the 27th August 1923. That's a record that is unlikely to ever be beaten.

A50. Sheffield Wednesday paid £1 million to Marseille for Chris Waddle in July 1992.

I hope you're learning some new facts about the Owls.

51. Who is the club's longest serving manager of all time?
    A. Rob Brown
    B. Jack Charlton
    C. Arthur Dickinson

52. Who is the club's longest serving post-war manager?
    A. Rob Brown
    B. Arthur Dickinson
    C. Eric Taylor

53. What is the name of the Sheffield Wednesday match day programme?
    A. The Owls Matchday Programme
    B. Wednesday
    C. Blue and White

54. Which of these is a Sheffield Wednesday fan's website?
    A. The Barn Owls
    B. The Owls Nest
    C. War of the Monster Trucks

55. Who is the current shirt sponsor?
    A. Azerbaijan Land of Fire
    B. Chansiri
    C. Host & Stay

56. Who was the club's first kit sponsor?
    A. Crosby Kitchens
    B. Finlux
    C. Topps Tiles

57. Which of these broadband companies have once sponsored the club?
    A. Demon
    B. Pipex
    C. PlusNet

58. Who was the club's first foreign signing?
    A. Des Hazel
    B. Klas Ingesson
    C. Ante Mirocevic

59. Who was the club's first black player?
    A. Deon Burton
    B. Tony Cunningham
    C. Drissa Diallo

60. Who was the club's first match in the league against?
    A. Blackburn Rovers
    B. Nottingham Forest
    C. Preston North End

Here are the answers to the last ten questions.

A51. Arthur Dickinson was the club's first ever manager starting in August 1891 and he is also the club's longest ever serving manager. He was manager of the club for 29 years, in charge for a staggering 919 games in total.

A52. Eric Taylor is the club's longest serving post war manager; in charge of 539 games in total before his retirement in July 1958.

A53. Wednesday is the imaginative name of the club's Matchday Programme.

A54. War of the Monster Trucks is a well-known Sheffield Wednesday fan's website. The rumour is that they are bringing back the paper fanzine, so we wish them well with that.

A55. Yorkshire based property management company Host & Stay are the current shirt sponsors.

A56. Wednesday's first sponsor was Crosby Kitchens, way back in 1981.

A57. PlusNet Broadband sponsored the club for four years from 2005 to 2009.

A58. Ante Mirocevic was the club's first foreign signing, way back in 1980. He got six caps for Yugoslavia.

A59. Jamaican Tony Cunningham was the club's first black player. He made 28 appearances, scoring four goals, in the 1984/85 season.

A60. Sheffield Wednesday's first league game was against Blackburn Rovers, on 12th September 1887.

Let's give you some easier questions.

61. What is the traditional colour of the home shirt?
    A. Blue and white stripes
    B. Green and white stripes
    C. Red and white stripes

62. What is the traditional colour of the away shirt?
    A. Red
    B. White
    C. Yellow

63. Who is considered as Sheffield Wednesday's main rivals?
    A. Barnsley
    B. Rotherham
    C. Sheffield United

64. What could be regarded as the club's most well-known song?
    A. Blue Moon
    B. Singing the Blues
    C. The Impossible Dream

65. What animal is on the club crest?
    A. Eagle
    B. Hawk
    C. Owl

66. How many seasons have Wednesday had in the Premier League?

A. 4
B. 6
C. 8

67. Who is currently the club chairman?
    A. Roman Abramovich
    B. Dejphon Chansiri
    C. Milan Mandaric

68. What nationality is the current club chairman?
    A. Malaysian
    B. Serbian
    C. Thai

69. In January 2015, the club was reportedly sold for how much?
    A. £17 million
    B. £27 million
    C. £37 million

70. What is the club's official twitter account?
    A. @OfficialSWFC
    B. @SWFC
    C. @Wednesday

Here are the answers to the last set of ten questions.

A61. The club's traditional home kit is blue and white stripes. Many supporters have been dismayed that the all blue strip the club have started wearing in the 2016/17 season is unlike anything worn previously in the club's long history.

A62. A tricky one as the club has adopted many different away kits over the years, but most say that the traditional away kit is either plain white or yellow. Give yourself a point for either answer.

A63. Obviously Sheffield United are the Owl's main rivals.

A64. "Singing the Blues" is a well-known Sheffield Wednesday song.

A65. It is of course an owl that is on the club's crest.

A66. Sheffield Wednesday were founder members of the Premier League, and spent eight consecutive seasons in the Premier League before their relegation at the end of the 1999/2000 season.

A67. Dejphon Chansiri is the club's current chairman. His net worth according to Forbes magazine is estimated to be approximately £500 million.

A68. Chansiri is a Thai business tycoon whose family owns Thai Union Frozen Group.

A69. Milan Mandaric sold the club in January 2015 to Chansiri for a figure close to £37 million. Chansiri has been reported as saying he is looking to sell the club.

A70. @SWFC is the official twitter account of the club. It tweets multiple times a day, and it deserves far more followers than it has.

Let's see how much you know about some of the club's players.

71. What shirt number did Paolo Di Canio wear?
    A. 7
    B. 10
    C. 11

72. Which goalkeeper holds the record for most appearances in goal for the club?
    A. Jack Brown
    B. Kevin Pressman
    C. Ron Springett

73. Just one Brazilian has played for the club. Who was it?
    A. Fabio
    B. Ramires
    C. Emerson Thome

74. How many times was Mark Bright the club's top goal scorer for the season?
    A. 2
    B. 3
    C. 4

75. How many times did Eric Potts win the supporters' Player of the Year?
    A. 1
    B. 2
    C. 3

76. How much did Sheffield Wednesday pay for David Hirst?
    A. £250,000
    B. £500,000
    C. £750,000

77. How many goals did David Hirst score for the club?
    A. 147
    B. 148
    C. 149

78. Who is the club's leading goal scorer in the Premier League?
    A. Mark Bright
    B. Paolo Di Canio
    C. David Hirst

79. What shirt number does Dominic Iorfa wear?
    A. 4
    B. 5
    C. 6

80. What sport did the club originally play?
    A. Cricket
    B. Hockey
    C. Rugby

Here are the answers to the last ten questions.

A71. Paolo Di Canio wore the number 11 shirt for Sheffield Wednesday, after joining the club from Celtic.

A72. Jack Brown appeared between the sticks an incredible 507 times between 1992 and 1937.

A73. Emerson Thome is the club's only Brazilian player, and he made a total of 62 appearances for the club.

A74. Mark Bright was the club's top goal scorer for three seasons in a row.

A75. Eric Potts won the supporters player for the year twice; in 1975 and 1976.

A76. Sheffield Wednesday paid £250,000 for David Hirst.

A77. David Hirst scored an impressive 149 goals for the club. A very impressive return on the money paid for him, I am sure you will agree.

A78. Mark Bright is the highest goal scorer for Wednesday in the Premier League to date, scoring 48 goals between 1992 and 1996.

A79. Defender Iorfa wears the number 6 shirt.

A80. Initially there was a cricket team named The Wednesday Cricket Club, after the day of the week they played their matches. The footballing side of the club was initially established to keep the team together and fit during the winter months.

Now some more questions about some of the club's managers over the years.

81. Who started the 2022/23 season as manager?
   A. Steve Bruce
   B. Garry Monk
   C. Darren Moore

82. Who was the club's first post-war manager?
   A. Harry Catterick
   B. Eric Taylor
   C. Billy Walker

83. Who was the club's first player-manager?
   A. Trevor Francis
   B. David Pleat
   C. Danny Wilson

84. Which of these Sheffield Wednesday managers has the highest win percentage?
   A. Vic Buckingham
   B. Harry Catterick
   C. Eric Taylor

85. How many times did Ron Atkinson manage the club?
   A. 1
   B. 2
   C. 3

86. How many Scottish managers have the club had?
    - A. 2
    - B. 3
    - C. 4

87. Who was the club's first Scottish manager?
    - A. Alan Irvine
    - B. Kimmy McMullan
    - C. Paul Sturrock

88. Which of these Howards once managed Sheffield Wednesday?
    - A. Howard Hughes
    - B. Howard Webb
    - C. Howard Wilkinson

89. Which Wednesday manager was in charge for the fewest number of games?
    - A. Ron Atkinson
    - B. Peter Eustace
    - C. Peter Shreeves

90. Who was the club's first manager from outside the UK?
    - A. Carlos Carvalhal
    - B. Jos Luhukay
    - C. Terry Yorath

Here are the answers to the last block of questions.

A81. Darren Moore started the 2022/23 season as manager. He was appointed to the role in March 2021.

A82. Eric Taylor was the club's first post-war manager; he managed the club up until 1958.

A83. Trevor Francis was the club's first player manager, taking over on 7th June 1991, the day after Ron Atkinson was sacked.

A84. Harry Catterick has the highest win percentage of any Sheffield Wednesday manager; with a very healthy win percentage of 55.8%.

A85. Ron Atkinson has managed the club twice.

A86. Sheffield Wednesday have had three Scottish managers.

A87. Kimmy McMullan was the club's first Scottish manager.

A88. Howard Wilkinson managed the club from June 1983 to October 1988. In his first season he guided the club to promotion to the First Division after a 14 year exile.

A89. Peter Eustace was only in charge of Sheffield Wednesday for 18 games.

A90. Portuguese Carlos Carvalhal was the club's first manager from outside the UK. He took over on 30th June 2015.

Here is the final set of questions.

91. When did Wednesday win the League Cup?
    A. 1990
    B. 1991
    C. 1992

92. Who did they beat in the final?
    A. Aston Villa
    B. Manchester City
    C. Manchester United

93. What was the score?
    A. 1-0
    B. 2-0
    C. 2-1

94. Who scored the winning goal?
    A. David Hirst
    B. John Sheridan
    C. Paul Williams

95. Who was the captain who lifted the trophy?
    A. Phil King
    B. Nigel Pearson
    C. Paul Williams

96. Who was the manager at the time?
    A. Ron Atkinson
    B. Trevor Francis
    C. Nigel Pearson

97. Who currently supplies the club's kit?
    A. Elev8
    B. Macron
    C. Sondico

98. Which of these sports brands have never
    supplied kit to Wednesday?
    A. Adidas
    B. Bukta
    C. Umbro

99. What position did the club finish at the end of
    the 2021/22 season?
    A. 4th
    B. 5th
    C. 6th

100. Who is the captain at the start of the 2022/23
     season?
     A. Barry Bannan
     B. Liam Palmer
     C. Josh Windass

101. Why are the club nicknamed the Owls?
     A. After Lord Owlton
     B. After a district of Sheffield
     C. After a very wealthy old factory owner

Here are the answers to the final set of questions.

A91. Sheffield Wednesday won the League Cup on the 21st April 1991.

A92. The Owls beat Manchester United in the 1991 League Cup Final.

A93. Sheffield Wednesday beat Manchester United 1-0 in front of 77,612 people at Wembley Stadium, and millions watching on TV.

A94. John Sheridan scored the only goal of the game in the 37th minute of the match.

A95. Captain Nigel Pearson lifted the trophy, and he was also voted the man of the match.

A96. Wednesday were managed by Ron Atkinson at the time.

A97. Macron are the official kit supplier.

A98. Adidas have never supplied kit to Wednesday, whereas both Bukta and Umbro, amongst others, have.

A99. The club finished 4th in League One last season.

A100. Barry Bannan started the 2022/23 as Sheffield Wednesday captain.

A101. Hillsborough is located in a north western part of the city called Owlerton, hence the nickname The Owls.

That's a nice question to finish with. I hope you enjoyed this ebook, and I hope you got most of the answers right. I also hope you learnt one or two new things about the club.

If you saw anything wrong, or have a general comment, please visit the glowwormpress.com website.

Thanks for reading, and if you did enjoy the book, would you please leave a positive review on Amazon.

Printed in Great Britain
by Amazon

18087412R00031